monuments

the delhi walla
monuments

mayank austen soofi

designed by solveig marina bang

First published in India in 2010 by Collins
An imprint of HarperCollins *Publishers*
a joint venture with
The India Today Group

ISBN: 978-93-5029-005-7

2 4 6 8 10 9 7 5 3 1

HarperCollins *Publishers*
A-53, Sector 57, NOIDA, Uttar Pradesh – 201301, India
77-85 Fulham Palace Road, London W6 8JB, United Kingdom
Hazelton Lanes, 55 Avenue Road, Suite 2900, Toronto,
Ontario M5R 3L2 and 1995 Markham Road, Scarborough,
Ontario M1B 5M8, Canada
25 Ryde Road, Pymble, Sydney, NSW 2073, Australia
31 View Road, Glenfield, Auckland 10, New Zealand
10 East 53rd Street, New York NY 10022, USA

Project Editor: Sheema Mookherjee
Typeset in Calisto MT 8/12

Printed and bound at
Gopsons Papers Ltd.

Contents

Old Delhi
(including Civil Lines)

ADMIT ONE

Red Fort
Mughal Kremlin

Where Opposite Chandni Chowk
Metro Stop Chandni Chowk
Open 9am-5pm (closed Mon)

Built in the 17th century by Shah Jahan

Red Fort or Lal Qila is that rare monument which encapsulates the essence of an entire historic timeline within its walls. The imperial court of the Mughals, it was built in the 17th century by Shah Jahan after he moved his capital from Agra to Delhi. The best of Mughal culture—poetry, music and cuisine—was created here.

Spread within a boundary of 2.41 km, the fort has its principal entry at Lahore Gate. The prime minister delivers his annual Independence Day speech from here. Immediately within the gate is the colonnaded **Meena Bazaar**, a tourist trap best avoided.

Guarding the entry to the palaces, the three-storeyed **Naubat Khana** gateway has carved designs on its walls, which were once painted with gold. Two later Mughal princes were murdered here. It now houses an Archaeological Survey of India office and the upper level has a war memorial museum. Beyond it, across the garden, is the **Diwan-i-Aam**, the hall of public audience.

7

OLD DELHI

Open on three sides, it has a white marble jharokha, overhanging balcony, under which the emperor sat. It was separated from the courtiers by a gold-plated railing. Today there is a transparent net instead.

Further along the garden pathway is a network of buildings that were the royal living quarters, now set amid colonial-era barracks (above). They once looked onto the river Yamuna but now the view is of the Ring Road.

Rang Mahal (right, below), the most prominent building, has its entrance barricaded but you can peek inside. It is difficult to imagine why it was called the palace of colours. The motifs are faded and the stone jaalis are broken. Some apartments here are called **Sheesh Mahal** (palace of mirrors), because their ceilings were decked with tiny mirrors.

In the centre flowed the neher-e-bhisht, stream of paradise. The canal, now dry, once carried cool water through a series of pavilions helping the Mughals survive the heat.

Next is **Khas Mahal**, the special palace. It housed the emperor's living room and bedroom. A marble screen hid the royal women in the zenana wing. In the adjacent **Diwan-i-Khas** (right, top) the emperor met his guests. The hall's ceiling was inlaid with gold and silver, vandalized in the twilight years of the Mughal Empire. On a marble pedestal stood the famous peacock throne, carried away to Persia by Nadir Shah after he sacked Delhi in 1739.

The **Hamam** (royal baths) and lovely **Moti Masjid** are closed to visitors. A corner museum boasts a manuscript by Maulana Rumi, some daggers and swords, and a few spotty paintings of the Mughals.

OLD
DELHI

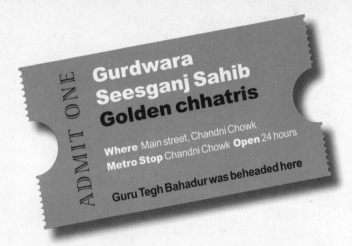

ADMIT ONE

Gurdwara Seesganj Sahib
Golden chhatris

Where Main street, Chandni Chowk
Metro Stop Chandni Chowk **Open** 24 hours

Guru Tegh Bahadur was beheaded here

Not as open and airy as Bangla Sahib Gurdwara in Connaught Place, Seesganj Sahib is as serene as any spiritual destination should be. It was built in memory of Guru Tegh Bahadur, the ninth Sikh guru who was beheaded here on the orders of Emperor Aurangzeb in 1675.

A three-storeyed rectangular building off the main street of Chandni Chowk, the gurdwara adds to the multi-religious character of Old Delhi's popular shopping district, which also has a mosque, a temple and a church.

The chaos of the bazaar disappears as you climb the short flight of stairs and reach a hall that hums with the devotional hymns of raagis, the musicians who sing in front of the Guru Granth Sahib, the Sikh holy book. The chandeliered hall has a carpeted marble floor where the devotees sit cross-legged with folded hands. On the terrace, the blare of auto rickshaw horns merges harmoniously with the tabla beats coming from inside the prayer hall. The balcony looks onto the bustling Bhai Mati Das Chowk.

Dating from the 17th century, the gurdwara has a small chhatri at each of its four corners and a large one at the centre. It has seen many additions and modifications. Langar (free kitchen) and lodging facilities are available for devotees. The halwa prasad is delicious and rich in ghee.

OLD
DELHI

ADMIT ONE

Fatehpuri Masjid
Unadorned tranquillity

Where Chandni Chowk
Metro Stop Chandni Chowk
Open Sunrise to sunset

Visit here in the twilight hours

A hidden getaway with few tourists or touts, its simplicity is magical. Fatehpuri Masjid, the Walled City's third largest mosque, is made of red sandstone.

The central dome looks as if it is made of marble, but is actually of lime mortar.

In a city of grand and imposing monuments, the plainness of this mosque is refreshing.

Tucked away at one end of Chandni Chowk, Old Delhi's signature street, the mosque's history is heavy with drama. It was commissioned in 1650 by Begum Fatehpuri, a wife of Shah Jahan.

Damaged by the British during the 1857 revolt, it was sold to a Hindu banker, only to be returned to Muslim ownership 20 years later.

Visit here during the twilight hours—the sky over the courtyard is a pale blue and the moon is newborn. Before the approaching night swallows the shade of the courtyard's giant ficus tree, the muezzin's call starts echoing from all sides.

Devotees stream in from the in-house madrasa and from the shops outside. All head first to the vazukhana, the little fish-filled water tank, for their ritual ablution.

As the men pray, the courtyard becomes as quiet as the 21 tombs clustered next to the tank. Calmness descends and Delhi disappears, although the bustle of Chandni Chowk is just outside the doorway.

FAST FACT The mosque was once sold to a Hindu banker

13

OLD DELHI

ADMIT ONE

Jain Svetambar Temple
Luxurious austerity

Where Naughara Street, Kinari Bazaar
Metro Stop Chandni Chowk
Open 6am-8pm (after hours ask caretaker)

Step in to discover unknown splendours

FAST FACT There is a museum of rare artifacts and manuscripts

Amid Delhi's dense tangle of mosques, forts and tombs, it is easy to miss the city's non-Islamic heritage. Don't let the Jain Svetambar Temple suffer this fate. The most beautiful Jain temple in the capital, it is lavishly decorated with intricate artwork. Tucked away at one end of a quiet alley, off the main lane of the noisy Kinari Bazaar, the triple-storeyed marble building dates from the late 18th century.

Inside you'll see priests dressed in pristine white (Svetambara means 'clad in white'). But the simplicity ends there as the devotional area on the first floor launches a delirious assault on the senses. The central courtyard overhanging with four huge chandeliers has exquisitely carved arches. At a corner sits the dramatic black image of Lord Parasnath (right), the 23rd tirthankara. In the sanctum sanctorum is the white marble statue of the chief deity—the fifth tirthankara (enlightened being), Sumatinath. He wears a silver crown, a diamond tilak on the forehead and a pure gold necklace. The dome is covered by gold leaves, while the silver-plated door opening into the shrine has an icon of Lakshmi.

The second floor is yet more flamboyant with wall-sized glass mosaics representing the life of Lord Mahavir. Restored in 2010, by the artist Zenul Khan (far right) from Rajasthan, using traditional paints, the dome is painted with figures of nobles, musicians and dancers. The museum on the ground floor has rare manuscripts, embroideries in gold thread and objects of pure silver. Worldly luxuries, Jain-style.

OLD
DELHI

Every 27 December, on the occasion of Ghalib's birthday, his admirers march to his haveli in Old Delhi with lighted candles and give sound bites to the media on the poet's relevance. As if he needs this lip service! What Shakespeare is to the English language, Mirza Ghalib (1797-1869) is to Urdu.

Mughal princes loved his works, as did roadside tipplers.

Today, Bollywood actors lip-sync his poetry and Indian politicians quote him in their speeches.

But nothing of the poet's popularity is reflected in the house where he spent his last nine years. Ghalib's last home lost its original flourishes of frescoes, alcoves and archways, following several sub-divisions and additions over the years.

Reduced to a dimly-lit gallery, a small verandah and

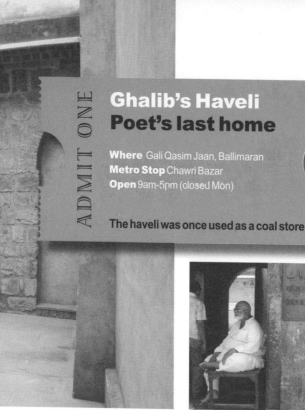

FAST FACT Also visit Ghalib's tomb in Nizamuddin. See p72

ADMIT ONE

Ghalib's Haveli
Poet's last home

Where Gali Qasim Jaan, Ballimaran
Metro Stop Chawri Bazar
Open 9am-5pm (closed Mon)

The haveli was once used as a coal store

a claustrophobic courtyard, it was a coal store at some time in the past.

Recent restoration has transformed the haveli into a makeshift museum with facsimiles of Ghalib's letters, some grainy pictures and, curiously, utensils of Ghalib's time. Apart from his books on display, a chart shows Ghalib's favourite dishes (bhuna gosht and sohan halwa).

The courtyard looks onto the back of a high-rise, the wall of which is spattered with paan stains and lined with sewage pipes. Ghalib would have chuckled at the setting.

These days not many Delhiites read Urdu and few care for poetry. But Ghalib immortalized the romance of 19th-century Delhi and anyone who feels for this city must pay this place a visit.

17

OLD
DELHI

ADMIT ONE

Razia Sultan's Tomb
Forgotten resting place

Where Pahari Bhojla, near Chitli Qabar
Metro Stop Chawri Bazaar
Open Sunrise to sunset

Quiet grave amid Old Delhi's teeming alleys

This tomb in a courtyard that lacks a roof or a dome is no resting place for a queen. It attracts no crowds and is no indicator of her legend. But that's the beauty of the place. As the first woman ruler of the Delhi Sultanate, as well as in South Asia, Razia (died 1240) rode elephants, fought in battlefields, loved a slave, married a rebel, and lost an empire.

This tomb 'believed to be of Razia', as an Archaeological Survey of India slab puts it, is like a tattered history book that lies forgotten in a jumble of the Walled City by-lanes.

Surrounded by brick apartments, the two crumbling stone mounds (the other said to be the tomb of Razia's sister) are relics waiting to be trampled over by the march of time. An interesting walk through shaded alleys teeming with chai stalls, hair salons and biryani joints, leads to the tomb's iron gate. Inside, a covered courtyard to the left serves as an impromptu mosque for locals.

Apart from the prayer hour, it is empty and peaceful. Try calling at the neighbouring houses to get access to their rooftops. The view is lovely.

OLD
DELHI

ADMIT ONE

Jama Masjid
Conference
of the birds

Where Old Delhi, opposite Urdu Bazaar
Metro Stop Chawri Bazaar
Open Sunrise to sunset (at prayer times only Muslims may enter)

Shah Jahan commissioned this mosque

Ask a filmmaker to close his eyes and think of Old Delhi, and most likely he will see the Jama Masjid. Built on a hillock, it is the Walled City's signature monument. Shah Jahan, who earlier created the Taj Mahal, commissioned this Friday mosque in 1650.

The main congregational masjid in the area, its courtyard has a full capacity of 25,000 worshippers. The balconies and platforms offer commanding views. The northern view looks to the Red Fort's ramparts; the south view exposes the Old Delhi skyline in all its delicious chaos—unpainted concrete structures, zigzagging

electrical wires, colourful hoardings, rickshaw carts and countless people.

But the courtyard itself is surprisingly serene, its quietness interrupted only by the cooing of pigeons flying intermittently to any of the three domes, and back. The spiritually inclined could consider sitting inside the prayer hall. You can also try climbing the mosque's southern minaret. The panoramic 360-degree view from the top is worth the climb up the dimly lit winding stairway.

Dress modestly. Women tourists are given capacious colourful kaftans to put on over their clothes.

21

OLD DELHI

The Sufi shrine of Hazrat Sarmad Shaheed is a bubble of serenity in an otherwise chaotic district. The noisy biryani sellers and quarrelsome beggars in the alley outside cannot disturb the quiet that prevails inside. Here you can achieve a Buddha-like calm. Nothing stirs the senses, not even the flaming red walls of the dargah. Everything—the tomb, the tiny courtyard, the sunlight and the occasional pilgrim—conspires to make you lose the concerns of the day.

But the shrine's patron saint lived a controversial life and died a violent death. Sarmad Shaheed was an Armenian Jew from Iran who converted to Islam.

22

ADMIT ONE

Sarmad Shaheed Dargah
Blood-red memorial

Where Opposite Gate No. 2, Jama Masjid
Metro Stop Chawri Bazaar
Open Sunrise to sunset

Aurangzeb ordered Sarmad's execution

He came to Sindh, fell in love with a Hindu boy, and then became a naked fakir before arriving in Delhi.

Here Mughal prince Dara Shikoh, the heir anointed, became his disciple. But history strummed its own tune. Aurangzeb, Dara's younger brother, rebelled against their father Shah Jahan, killed Dara, and was crowned emperor. Soon after Sarmad was executed on Aurangzeb's orders.

All this bloodshed seems to have now been forgotten within the blood-red walls of the dargah.

Devotees arrive, pray, make wishes, meditate, doze off, wake up, go away, and come back again.

OLD DELHI

ADMIT ONE

Nicholson Cemetery
Weep not

Where Near Kashmiri Gate bus terminus
Metro Stop Kashmiri Gate
Open Sunrise to sunset

Discover graves of the British killed in 1857

It is a mystery why guidebooks have been indifferent to the (deathly) charms of one of Delhi's oldest British cemeteries. Guarded by a cross-shaped gateway, Nicholson Cemetery has a sloping, grassy landscape dotted with tombstones, some intricately carved, some stark and simple.

Neem, date and tamarind trees watch over like sentinels, while thick bougainvilleas, weighed down with flowers, shed pink petals over the graves of 'dearly loved' children and 'beloved' spouses.

The personal details of the departed are preceded by carefully chosen poems or Biblical verses. One tomb inscription reads: Jesus said, 'weep not'.

Stone angels look over your shoulder as you try to decipher these engravings after sweeping away the dry leaves that cover them.

Some tombstones display curious symbols indicating the deceased's profession, while many graves date from the 1857 uprising. The cemetery's most prominent grave is that of its namesake Brigadier General John Nicholson, who was nicknamed 'the Lion of Punjab'. An Irish army officer in the British East India Company, Nicholson died of wounds received during the revolt. His tomb lies near the entrance, barricaded by an iron grill that is invaded by jasmine vines.

On the far side, towards the Ring Road, marigolds adorn the new graves of Indian Christians.

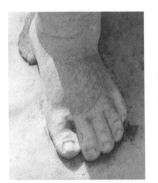

CIVIL LINES

ADMIT ONE

St James' Church
Battlefield promise

Where Near Kashmere Gate
Metro Stop Kashmere Gate
Sunday services 8am (Apr-Sep),
8.30am (Oct-Mar)

Built by military adventurer James Skinner

The first church to be built by the British in Delhi, St James' has a comfortingly small interior. The roof doesn't soar and the altar doesn't seem too far from the entrance. Unlike some other Delhi churches, where the scale of the architecture is majestic, here you feel as though you are in a neighbourhood chapel.

The church was built in 1836. Its dome rests on an octagonal arcade and the parishioners sit in the circular space below. Above the altar, on either side of the cross, two stained-glass windows depict the crucifixion and ascension.

Immediately below the communion table lies the tombstone of Colonel James Skinner, the military adventurer who lent his name to the church. Son of a Scottish army officer and a Rajput mother, Skinner is known for the two cavalry regiments he raised for the British Army in India. In 1800, while lying wounded in a battlefield, he promised to build a church if he survived and St James' was the result.

St James' was the Viceroy's Church until the Cathedral Church of Redemption was built in 1931.

On the north side of the compound is the family graveyard of the Skinners where many of the colonel's 14 wives and children are buried.

The compound also has graves of other important British personalities such as William Fraser and Thomas Metcalfe.

CIVIL LINES

Central Delhi

(including East Delhi)

CENTRAL DELHI

Khooni Darwaza

Firoz Shah Kotla Ruins

Purana Qila

Agrasen Baoli

Jantar Mantar

Sacred Heart Cathedral

Bangla Sahib Gurdwara

Lakshmi Narain Temple

Teen Murti Bhavan

Indira Gandhi Memorial

Cathedral Church of the Redemption

Raisina Hill

Lodhi Garden

EAST DELHI

Akshardham Temple

ADMIT ONE

Khooni Darwaza

Headless ghosts

Where Opposite Maulana Abul Kalam Medical College, Bahadur Shah Zafar M

Metro Stop Pragati Maidan

Open Sunrise to sunset

Restless spirits are said to ha

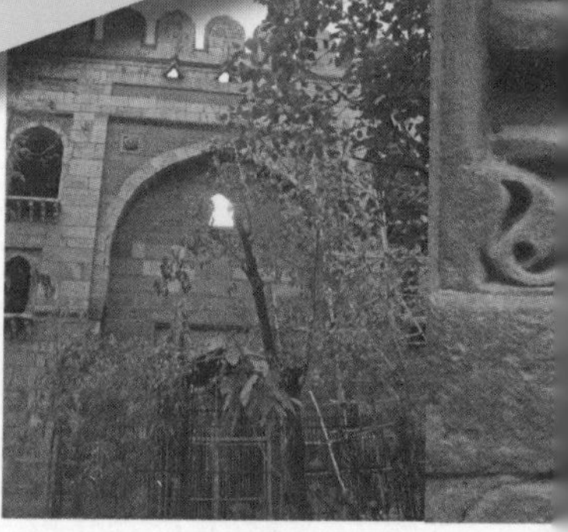

Khooni Darwaza means 'bloodied gateway' and legend has it that blood drips from its ceilings during the monsoon. Built by Sher Shah Suri in 1540 it is in the middle of the four-lane Bahadur Shah Zafar Marg connecting New and Old Delhi. It was originally named Kabuli Darwaza, when Kabul-bound caravans left the city through its arched entrance.

The gateway, 15.5m high, took its present name after the Mughals started displaying the heads of executed criminals from its battlements. Soon it became a popular place to hang the body parts of unwanted princes. Emperor Aurangzeb displayed his brother Dara's head at the gate.

After the British crushed the 1857 uprising, they killed the sons of the last Mughal, Bahadur Shah Zafar, at this gateway. It is believed that the restless spirits of Zafar's sons still float around in the ruin.

But snooping around this ghoulish monument is not so easy. The staircases reaching three different levels within the gate are closed to visitors. So good luck with your ghost spotting.

29

CENTRAL DELHI

ADMIT ONE

Firoz Shah Kotla Ruins
The fifth city

Where Near ITO crossing,
Bahadur Shah Zafar Marg
Metro Stop Pragati Maidan
Open Sunrise to sunset

A replica mosque was built in Samarkand

Built as the citadel of Firoz Shah Tughlaq, along the banks of the Yamuna, this is now a ruin. Firozabad, the fifth city of Delhi, once extended from Hauz Khas to Pir Ghaib (near Bara Hindu Rao hospital), but most of the buildings were vandalized during the construction of the new city of Shahjahanabad.

This is one of the few Delhi ruins that is not patronized by tourists or romantic couples. The once-scenic gateways lead to nowhere and the stairs go up to gloomy circular chambers.

Squirrels race up the stone ramparts and colonies of pigeons and parakeets fly out of reach of the numerous cats. On Thursday nights people who believe they are possessed by djinns come to the chambers beneath the mosque to be exorcised by Sufis.

The Jami Masjid, raised on a platform, is entered through a domed gateway. It has hardly any ornamentation left. The walls on its east and north have disappeared. Standing amid its ruinous state, it is difficult to imagine that the 14th-century invader Timur was so impressed by it that he created a replica in his hometown, Samarkand.

Facing the masjid is the 80m-high Ashokan pillar, one of a series of columns erected by the Mauryan king in the 3rd century BC. It stands on a three-storeyed pyramid made of rubble, with small chambers on each level.

Transplanted from its original site in Punjab, the astonishingly smooth pillar, with its clear inscription, is one thing here that does not look ruined.

CENTRAL DELHI

Legend attributes Delhi's founding thousands of years ago to the Pandavas of the Mahabharata. The site of their capital, Indraprastha, is now home to Purana Qila, the Old Fort, an imposing sight on Mathura Road often ignored by city commuters. But do not discount the 4m-thick, 20m-high and over a mile-long rampart of Purana Qila.

After all it was the creation of Sher Shah Suri who gave South Asia its first great highway, the Grand Trunk Road. The fort's **Qila-i-Kohna Masjid** (1542) is one of the most elegant mosques in Delhi.

Facing a garden, its five entrance arches increase in size towards the centre in an imperceptible way. Inside, the mihrabs (recesses) on the

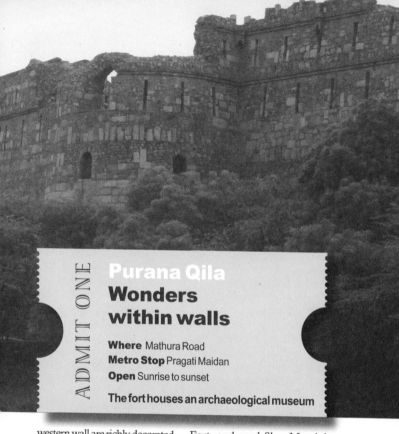

ADMIT ONE

Purana Qila
Wonders within walls

Where Mathura Road
Metro Stop Pragati Maidan
Open Sunrise to sunset

The fort houses an archaeological museum

western wall are richly decorated with Quranic inscriptions and circular patterns. The dome displays the remnants of blue and yellow glazed tiles.

Close by is **Sher Mandal** (inset). Topped by a chhatri, it is an octagonal building with two layers of deeply depressed arches. After Sher Shah's death, Mughal emperor Humayun reclaimed Delhi and the Old Fort, and used Sher Mandal as his library. One evening he slipped on its stairs and died.

The fort also houses a hamam (bath), a baoli (well), three beautiful gateways and an archaeological museum. There is a landscaped park next to Bara Darwaza, the entrance gate. Outside, the moat set against the majestic fort walls is one of Delhi's most scenic sights.

FAST FACT Site of Indraprastha

33

CENTRAL DELHI

Agrasen Baoli
Cool refuge

Where Hailey Road, Connaught Place
Metro Stop Barakhamba
Open 9am-5pm

Once a summer shelter of the heat-stricken

Amid the business towers and residential apartments of Connaught Place, this 14th century baoli or ancient step-well, is flanked on both sides by niches, chambers and passageways, and the 104 stone steps descending into the well's dried-up base, have three levels. It is not certain who built it, though some credit it to a king called Agrasen; hence the name.

As you enter, you will see a mosque on one side. Initially, you will hear the cooing of hundreds of pigeons. But as you walk down the stairs, the silence deepens, the city skyline disappears and the daylight fades away.

This was a reservoir, as well as a summer refuge, for heat-stricken citizens living in pre-Lodhi times. As the water level receded each summer, the people would seek a cool retreat in the baoli's lower reaches. There was water (and filth) here until 2002. Boys swam, lovers threw wish-making coins … and the depressed jumped. But the popularity of this well, spanning 60 m in length and 15 m in width, has evaporated with its water.

Its solitude is remarkable, but that is a pity in some ways. Here is a beautiful relic that has survived in a time capsule and is holding its own against urbanization, and yet its magnificence lies unacknowledged.

CENTRAL
DELHI

ADMIT ONE

Jantar Mantar
Giant sundial

Where Parliament Street, Connaught Place
Metro Stop Rajiv Chowk
Times 9am–5pm

A picturesque observatory

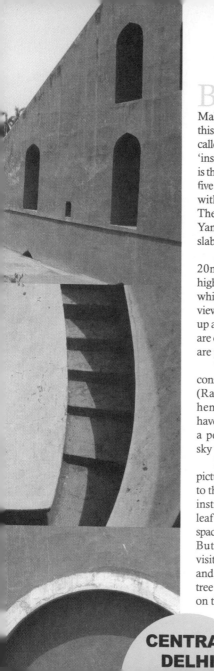

Built in the early 1700s by the founder of Jaipur, Maharaja Sawai Jai Singh II, this observatory was originally called Yantra Mantra, meaning 'instruments and formulae'. It is these yantra that make up the five most prominent landmarks within a landscaped garden. The central building, Samrat Yantra, is a giant quadrangular slab of rubble masonry.

Ascending to more than 20m, its stairs look to the highrises of Connaught Place, which now sadly block out its view of the skies. Boys running up and down the sloping walls are only faintly aware that they are playing on a sundial.

The two other yantra, consisting of circular buildings (Ram) and complementary hemispheres (Jai Prakash), have adequate appeal to excite a person with no interest in sky watching.

Misra Yantra, the most picturesque structure, is closest to the entrance. A mix of four instruments, it has a 'peepal leaf look' and is conveniently spacious for group photo shoots. But the truth is that most visitors don't care for the sun and stars. Lovers etch vows on tree trunks and tourists lounge on the grass.

FAST FACT Misra Yantra, the most striking structure, is a combination of four instruments

37

CENTRAL DELHI

Sacred Heart Cathedral
Hall of grace

Where Opp Gol Dak Khana, near Connaught Place **Metro Stop** Rajiv Chowk
Sunday mass Summer: 6.30am, 9am, 11.30am, 6.30pm. Winter: 6.30am, 9am, 11.30am, 6pm

Headquarters of the Delhi Archdiocese

Delhi's largest Catholic church has twice been graced by the presence of Pope John Paul II.

Spread over 14 acres, which includes two schools, the cathedral is the headquarters of the Delhi Archdiocese. Completed in 1934, it was built 70 years after the city's first Catholic church, St Mary's, near Delhi railway station.

Henry Medd, who later became the chief architect to the government of British India, designed it. The red brick structure was selected from eight entries that were judged by a panel which included Edwin Lutyens.

The church has a massive vaulted ceiling under a towering curved roof, polished stone floors and broad arches. The façade has plaster mouldings and cupolas.

The dark arches of the entrance enhance the building's immensity. The altar is domed and made of pure Carrara marble.

The main fresco of Christ and his 12 disciples (who have green eyebrows and blue hair) is painted by an unknown artist. The artwork shows signs of age but still looks glorious.

The archbishop of Agra, who also laid the building's foundation, presented the bell, vestments and altar furniture.

On Sundays, hymns are sung to the accompaniment of an electronic keyboard and services are offered in more than one language.

Lepers and memento-sellers crowd the iron gate outside. The worshippers thronging Sacred Heart Cathedral during Christmas Eve cause traffic jams each year.

FAST FACT The design was selected from among eight entries judged by Edwin Lutyens

39

CENTRAL DELHI

ADMIT ONE

Bangla Sahib Gurdwara
Reflections of faith

Where Opp Gol Dak Khana, near Connaught Place **Metro Stop** Rajiv Chowk
Open 24 hours

Dedicated to Guru Har Krishan

Built by a Sikh general in 1783, this gurdwara has an expansive compound and a large sarovar (holy pond). Dedicated to Guru Har Krishan, the eighth Sikh guru, it was so named because it is on the site of the bungalow of the Mughal nobleman, Mirza Raja Jai Singh, where the guru stayed during a visit to Delhi in 1664. The gold-plated dome reflects beautifully in the pond, which teems with goldfish.

A corridor, skirting its entire length, has a small white dome on each corner. Up the stairs from the pond is a marbled courtyard with a nishan sahib, a tall flagpole that marks every

gurdwara. This traditional symbol of Sikh identity is draped in a saffron cloth and topped by a two-edged dagger, and worshippers flock to pay respects to it.

Inside the prayer hall raagis sing with their harmoniums and tablas all day long, as a priest fans the Guru Granth Sahib. Devotees sit cross-legged, lost in their own thoughts. The hall's upper floor has glass-panelled cabins where scholars read the holy book.

The gurdwara's famous langar offers puffy rotis, earthy dal, subzi and piping hot kheer at a sit-down meal at regular intervals..

CENTRAL DELHI

Lakshmi Narain Temple
Vishnu's land

Where Mandir Marg, near Gol Market
Metro Stop Patel Chowk
Open 4.30am-1.30pm and 2.30pm-9pm

Includes shrine to Sai Baba

FAST FACT The temple is also known as the Birla Mandir

Spread over seven acres, Shri Lakshmi Narain Temple, popularly called Birla Mandir, is a dense neighbourhood of gods. A world in itself, it is a land of plenty. It has shops, phone booths, photo studios, a dispensary and a dharamshala (guesthouse). It has fruit trees, streams, fountains, bridges and rocks. But it's the brick-red temple tower (165 feet high) that takes your breath away.

While the presiding deity is Vishnu, Birla Mandir advocates the philosophy of monotheism and is open to all faiths. Built by the Birla family, it was inaugurated by Mahatma Gandhi in 1939 in the presence of Jugal Kishoreji Birla, whose statue stands in a hedged garden.

The chief prayer hall is beautiful, airy and tranquil. Pigeons hover around the large chandelier. Nearby, there is a giant globe and a huge bell on the floor. The marble walls are etched with figures of gods and inscribed with shlokas. Elephant heads are sculpted

on the ceiling. The path of parikrama, the anti-clockwise circumambulation around the deity, passes through a mirror-lined gallery.

The temple's backyard is landscaped with statues of gods, kings, holy men and animals. Artificial caves can be entered through the jaws of a crocodile and a lion. Sheshnag, the serpent god, stands in the centre of a pond. A stone pillar is carved with images of the historical warriors Rani Lakshmi Bai and Maharana Pratap.

To see the crowd, try your luck at Sai Baba's shrine within the temple complex. Surrounded by humankind, birds and beasts (so what if they are in stone), you feel yourself to be a part of the world and yet removed from it.

The more worldly visitors can scavenge the souvenir stores for postcards, bangles, statues and religious music.

There is a special reception hall for foreigners and cameras are not allowed in the main temple.

CENTRAL DELHI

ADMIT ONE

Teen Murti Bhavan
In remembrance

Where Teen Murti Marg
Metro Stop Patel Chowk
Open 9am-5pm (closed Mon)

The planetarium is housed here

FAST FACT Spread over 45 acres

Designed by the English architect Robert Tor Russel, who also designed Connaught Place, Teen Murti Bhavan (1930) is fittingly dedicated to India's most Anglophile statesman, Jawaharlal Nehru.

Built for the commander-in-chief of the British Indian Army, the stately mansion was the residence of Jawaharlal Nehru who lived here until his death in 1964.

A few months later the massive 30-room residence was turned into a museum. Spread over 45 acres, gardens included, the mansion is filled with old-world elegance.

Musty books line the corridors. Family portraits of the Nehru-Gandhi family deck the walls. Grand staircases, wood-panelled galleries and low-hanging ceiling fans add to the character.

Drawing rooms and

bedrooms look so ready-to-use that you half expect Nehru to tap you on the shoulder.

The occasional sound in the sprawling gardens is of the peacock's call. Squirrels scurry through the leaf-strewn grass. Around the inexpensive museum canteen, the surrounding star fruit and wood apple trees serve as natural air conditioners.

The museum also has a planetarium. It is a pity that the excellent library is open only to accredited research scholars. In the roundabout outside the mansion stand the famous three statues—or the teen murtis that give the place its name—representing the princely states of Hyderabad, Mysore and Jodhpur and dedicated to Indian soldiers who died in the Middle East during the First World War.

Installed within a landscaped garden, they were sculptured by Leonard Jennings.

45

ADMIT ONE

**Indira Gandhi
Memorial**
A simple reminder

Where 1 Safdarjung Road
Metro Stop Patel Chowk
Times 9am-5pm (closed Mon)

Relics of the Nehru-Gandhi family

The memorial to India's first woman prime minister is at her former residence, where she was assassinated by her own bodyguards in 1984. But it is more than a museum. Besides showing the usual bedrooms, dining room, library, and even the last sari worn by the powerful politician, once described as 'the only man in her cabinet', the house is also a window into the world of the famed Lutyens' bungalows.

Built during the twilight years of the British Empire, there are 800 such bungalows spread over 550 hectares in New Delhi. Responsible for giving the city much of its colonial-era charm, most of these elegant white houses have been taken over by politicians and bureaucrats and so are barred to the public.

Marked by wide, open verandahs that keep the inner rooms shielded from Delhi's searing summer sun, these bungalows have high ceilings that carry the hot air up to be whisked away through the ventilators. Creepers climb the walls, potted plants deck the doorways and the disproportionately large wooded gardens ward off claustrophobia.

After Mrs Gandhi's assassination, her son, Rajiv, became prime minister. The family lived here for a few months before leaving for a nearby bungalow at 7 Race Course Road. The house was then thrown open to tourists. While most rooms in the museum were left unchanged, some were emptied to make way for newspaper clippings, framed pictures and relics of the Nehru-Gandhi dynasty.

The decor in the book-lined rooms is simple, yet tasteful. There is one exception: a glass case that displays the shreds of a kurta that Rajiv Gandhi was wearing when he was assassinated in 1991. The sight is disturbing.

CENTRAL DELHI

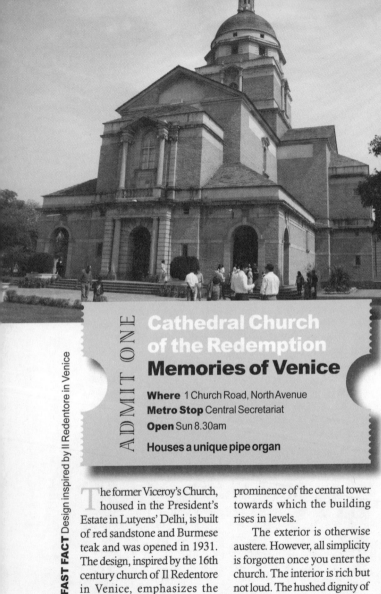

ADMIT ONE

Cathedral Church of the Redemption
Memories of Venice

Where 1 Church Road, North Avenue
Metro Stop Central Secretariat
Open Sun 8.30am

Houses a unique pipe organ

The former Viceroy's Church, housed in the President's Estate in Lutyens' Delhi, is built of red sandstone and Burmese teak and was opened in 1931. The design, inspired by the 16th century church of Il Redentore in Venice, emphasizes the prominence of the central tower towards which the building rises in levels.

The exterior is otherwise austere. However, all simplicity is forgotten once you enter the church. The interior is rich but not loud. The hushed dignity of

the carpeted floor harmonizes smoothly with the dazzling interplay of the arches.

The small recessed openings in the sidewalls let in beams of sunlight that make the otherwise dark nave feel mystical. The altar faces the east and is capped by a half dome. Above is a copy of the *Madonna and Child* by the 15th-century Italian Renaissance painter Giovanni Bellini.

The choir gallery over the western entrance boasts a unique William Hill, Norman & Beard pipe organ, which was installed for a princely sum of Rs 34,825, a fortune at the time.

Initially, the building suffered from bad acoustics and there was an unwanted reverberation. But in 1934 the ceiling of the dome was coated with asbestos solution to rectify the problem. This finally enabled the magnificent teakwood organ to give the cathedral the beautiful music that it deserved.

On festival days, surrounded by bright bulbs and forests of gladioli, you can sit among a remarkably diverse throng and sing hymns with gusto.

49

Raisina Hill
We, the people

Where Around India Gate **Metro Stop** Central Secretariat **Open** The avenues have open access day and night.

Flanked by South Block and North Block

The architectural showcase of India's ruling elite, Raisina Hill is an empire fashioned out of sandstone. In the early 20th century, a village of this name was relocated by the British to build Viceroy House, which was renamed Rashtrapati Bhavan upon becoming the official residence of the Indian president. The exterior of the complex is a must-see.

The best way to approach Raisina Hill is to start your walk, or car ride, from India Gate, the 1,938 foot-high memorial arch, India's 'Arc de Triomphe', designed by Edwin Landseer Lutyens in 1931.

With the names of 13,516 officers, who died fighting at the North-West Frontier and in the Third Afghan War, etched on its arch, India Gate looks best in the dawn light.

The memorial is connected to Rashtrapati Bhavan by the 2.4km-long Rajpath, the principal route of the annual parade on Republic Day.

As you walk up the Raisina Hill, the approaching Rashtrapati Bhavan begins to disappear from view.

51

CENTRAL
DELHI

By the time you reach the vast square of Vijay Chowk, you only see the dome.

On the left of Rajpath is the South Block, the office of the external affairs and defence ministries; on the right is the North Block, which houses the finance and home ministry. Despite the Orwellian-sounding names, these are scenic buildings with pillars and domes. They were designed not by Lutyens, but by Herbert Baker, who worked with him.

The most arresting sight, however, is the Rashtrapati Bhavan. The closest point you can reach is the ornate gate. Spread over 20,000 sq m, the president's house has 340 rooms, 37 reception rooms, 74 lobbies and galleries and 18 staircases. In the backdrop of the sinking sun, the giant columns of this massive edifice turn into papery silhouettes. Entry is opened once a year in spring, at the famous Mughal Gardens.

Pictured above: India Gate being spruced up for the Commonwealth Games; left: women at India Gate during Chhat Puja.

CENTRAL DELHI

The present-day perception of Lodhi Garden is of well-kept flowerbeds, exotic trees and green sloping lawns scattered with monuments. Few know that the structures long precede the garden, which was created in 1936 on the site of a village called Khairpur. The tombs were erected by the Sayyids (1414-51) and Lodhis (1451-1526) and make dramatic centrepieces in this peaceful oasis in the heart of the city.

Visible from Lodhi Road, **Muhammad Shah Sayyid's**

Lodhi Garden
Landscaped tombs

Where Lodhi Road
Open 6am-8pm

The garden was created in 1936

mausoleum, stands on an elevated mound. One of Delhi's earliest octagonal tombs, it is the only one of its kind with no walled compound; perhaps the money ran out or the walls collapsed. Surrounded by royal palms it has a verandah running around it, with three arched openings on each of its eight sides.

The second octagonal tomb in Lodhi Garden is over the **grave of Sikandar Lodhi** (left). This 16th-century ruler of the Afghan Lodhi dynasty was a handsome and brave man, but also ruthless and bigoted. Perhaps that dual personality is reflected in the tomb. While artistic coloured tiles deck the interiors and chhatris, its outer wall resembles fort-like ramparts. Commissioned by Sikandar's son, Ibrahim, in 1517, it is the earliest surviving enclosed garden tomb in India.

At the centre are two unknown tombs. Built of dressed stone, **Bara Gumbad** (above) is a group of three buildings. The central structure with its

FAST FACT The tombs of the Lodhis and Sayyids are found here

55

red sandstone ornamentation, arched recess and decorative battlements is shaped like a tomb although there is no grave. The interior of the adjacent mosque (far right) is rich in arabesque stucco décor, Quranic inscriptions and geometric designs. There are remnants of painted work on the ceiling.

In contrast, the facing pavilion, **Mehman Khana**, (guest house), presumably for pilgrims, is bare and monastic.

Directly opposite the Bara Gumbad lies the more sunny **Sheesh Gumbad**. Its dome was originally embellished with blue enamelled tiles; hence its name, meaning 'glazed dome'. The inside chamber is gloomy and it houses several unknown graves.

The **Athpula bridge** (right), close to the garden's main entrance, is one of the few surviving structures built in Delhi during Akbar's reign. It once spanned a tributary of the Yamuna, but today its seven arches overlook several fountains.

CENTRAL
DELHI

Akshardham Temple
Tomorrow's heritage

ADMIT ONE

Where Near Noida Modh
Metro Stop Yamuna Bank
Open 10am-7pm (Apr-Sep), 9am-6pm
(Oct-Mar), (closed Mon)

Musical fountain and boat rides

It's over the top. Swaminarayan Akshardham temple complex is like a theme park. According to *The New York Times*, the temple has a 'Disney touch' and that's no exaggeration. Akshardham boasts a musical fountain, a large-format movie screen and boat rides, among other things—all coming with a fee.

Offering a mix of religious and nationalist paraphernalia, it has statues of sadhus as well as 'patriots of India'. Built over 100 acres on the banks

of the Yamuna, the temple is dedicated to the 18th-century sage, Bhagwan Swaminarayan, who at the age of 11 embarked on a spiritual journey across the subcontinent and has an enormous following in India and abroad.

Don't expect to achieve much spiritual calm here. There is a constant crowd of people streaming through. But if you don't tire easily, the place is entertaining. The temple, the chief attraction, is built of pink sandstone and white marble. It has nine domes, 20 pinnacles, 234 pillars and over 20,000 sculptured figures.

In the centre is a gold-plated statue of Bhagwan Swaminarayan, that stands on a plinth embellished with 148 elephants. The surrounding two-tier colonnade has over 2,000 pillars and 300 windows.

There is also a food court and souvenir shop. No other temple in Delhi is as grand as this.

FAST FACT 148 elephants grace the temple

EAST DELHI

South Delhi

ADMIT ONE

Safdarjung's Tomb
Faded glory

Where Aurobindo Marg, near AIIMS
Open Sunrise to sunset

A spectacle in marble and pink sandstone

The mausoleum of Mughal aristocrat Safdarjung (1754), with its stained sandstone walls and insufficient marble, reflects the twilight years of a great empire.

Considered to be the last large Mughal building built in India (the first being Humayun's Tomb), the marble used on the onion dome was stripped from the nearby tomb of an early Mughal noble called Abdul Rahim Khan-i-Khana. But the loot was not enough and so pink sandstone was used to finish off the incomplete patches of white. Despite the mix, the final look has a certain dignity-in-decline grace.

The large and windy double-storeyed gateway has a library and a verandah upstairs. The little mosque on the doorway's

right is handsome, but is closed to visitors.

A pathway lined with bottle palm trees leads to the tomb. Made of red and buff sandstone, it lies in the middle of a garden. The platform on which it stands has a series of cells with locked wooden doors. The tomb's pillars are ornamental, their tops ending in elegant jharokhas. The tomb chamber displays excessively ornate, almost kitschy, plaster decoration. The rooms around it have windows with views of the garden.

Built by the Nawab Shujauddaulah, Safdarjung's son, the tomb is mostly visited by lovers who want to escape the city's prying eyes.

61

SOUTH DELHI

Khan-i-Khana's Tomb
Scarred beauty

Where Nizamuddin East
Open Sunrise to sunset

Neglected tomb set in a spacious garden

A stone-paved lane, hedged with marigold bushes, leads to one of Delhi's strangest monuments. The 16th-century tomb of the Mughal noble, Abdul Rahim Khan-i-Khana, is both ugly and beautiful.

Its exterior stonework has been stripped off. The plaster on the inside walls is chipped and the niches are cobwebbed. The ceilings are covered with romantic graffiti.

But before you notice the flaws, the weathered dome, as well as the chhatris and arches, make a strong impact on you.

The underground tomb is inaccessible, and the sarcophagus in the upper chamber is bare, quiet and dark.

Bordered by the tony Nizamuddin East bungalows on one side and the noisy Mathura Road on the other,

the large garden around the tomb is like a city getaway. It is dotted with trees and in the mornings the neighbourhood's health-conscious inhabitants treat it like their very own Lodhi Garden.

Besides being Akbar's prime minister, Khan-i-Khana translated Babur's memoirs from Chaghatai to Persian. He composed poetry, wrote two books on astrology and had a good command of Sanskrit. There is a verse written on him by Tulsidas.

FAST FACT Khan-i-Khana was Akbar's prime minister and was a great scholar

SOUTH DELHI

ADMIT ONE

Humayun's Tomb
Postcard perfect

Where Near Mathura Rd
Open 9am-7pm

Set in an exquisite 30-acre garden

Supposedly the first draft of Taj Mahal, Humayun's Tomb is perfect in its unearthly beauty. Visitors are transported into a world of calendar art as they step into a compound seemingly untouched by time. Built in 1565 by Humayun's widow, Hamida Banu Begum, the garden tomb has over 100 graves, including those of two of his queens and of Dara Shikoh who was interred here after being murdered by his brother, Aurangzeb. In 1857, Bahadur Shah Zafar was captured here by the British before being exiled to Burma.

The mausoleum's 47m-high platform looks onto a Sikh gurdwara and a Buddhist stupa. The earliest elaborate example of Mughal architecture, it was the first time that marble and sandstone were used in such great quantities in India. The side chambers have sandstone jaalis through which the sun's rays make intricate patterns.

The 30-acre garden is picture perfect with its careful maintenance. The fountains work, the hedges are pruned and even the trees look trimmed. Sit on the benches to listen to the sound of birds chattering, the distant rumble of a train and the tourist conversation.

65

SOUTH CENTRAL

Or just watch the squirrels play games with each other. In case you are hungry, there's an extremely modest canteen next to the entrance.

After the immensity of Humayun's Tomb, it is calming to confront the relative smallness of **Afsarwala Makbara**, the officer's tomb. Nobody knows who was buried here or when exactly it was built, though it is an early Mughal-period octagonal building.

While the wilderness around its red sandstone façade has been trimmed into a garden, the tomb's untamed nature refuses to subside. In the twilight hour, the gathering darkness makes its unremarkable beauty poignant. It faces the canteen and has a mosque (above right) on its side.

Behind is the walled enclosure of **Arab Serai** that housed the Persian craftsmen who came to build Humayun's Tomb. The serai's gateway is noted for its jharokhas that display the leftovers of what must have been a beautiful arrangement of glazed ceramic tiles.

The gate looks lovelier from inside, as the centuries have softened the edges of the stones. While entering the complex, you will encounter the **tomb of Isa Khan** (right), which is so attractive that uninformed tourists occasionally mistake it

for Humayun's tomb. Isa Khan was a noble in the court of Humayun's nemesis Sher Shah Suri. His octagonal tomb has sloping buttresses that give it its signature look of strength. There is glazed tile work on the arches and chhatris on the roof.

The bordering mosque with some well-preserved tile work offers a wide-angle view of the tomb.

SOUTH
DELHI

Nizamuddin Dargah
Among the Sufis

Where Nizamuddin Basti
Open 5am-10pm

Much to explore in this dargah complex

This bustling dargah complex has tombs, domes, music, poetry, pilgrims, shops and some say, even djinns. Delhi's most touristy Sufi destination has grown around the tomb of 14th-century mystic, Nizamuddin Auliya, and is one of South Asia's most sacred Islamic shrines. The main entrance is through a dark winding alley that skirts an ancient baoli and opens into the shrine's marble courtyard. Here are buried saints and musicians, kings and princesses.

Nothing remains of the original Nizamuddin tomb chamber. The silence of his grave, the sight of people praying around it, the old-world costumes of the dargah's caretakers, all conjure up an air that can make even a non-believer feel meditative. Sitting here quietly is an intense spiritual experience. The inquisitive traveller will find a lot to explore.

FAST FACT One of South Asia's most sacred Islamic shrines

SOUTH
DELHI

Other monuments in the complex include the red sandstone **Jamaat Khana mosque** (left), the courtyard's oldest monument. Built by a son of Allauddin Khilji in 1325, it has Quranic inscriptions on the archways, pigeon-lined parapets and two side rooms where you can take a nap.

Try not to skip **Jahanara's Tomb** (below) that is adjacent to the mosque. Daughter of Shah Jahan and a Nizamuddin devotee, her wish was to be buried under an unadorned tomb opening onto the sky.

Most likely you will find flowers on Jahanara's grave, with a solitary pilgrim dozing off nearby, or even having a biryani feast. A marble screen separates it from the courtyard.

A more adventurous experience is the adjoining grave of **Muhammad Shah Rangeela**, another member of the Mughal royalty. His tomb is usually claimed by emotionally disturbed pilgrims shaking and swirling their heads, asking the spirit to leave their bodies.

Right behind is the tomb of **Amir Khusro**, one of the most popular disciples of Nizamuddin. The tradition is to visit his tomb first. Having made such a significant contribution to Hindustani classical music, Khusro's tomb could not be at a better place, musically speaking. The courtyard reverberates with qawalis in the evenings, with a special performance on Thursdays. The qawwals are descendants of a family who have been singing here for the last 750 years and attending a session can be quite an out-of-body experience.

71

ADMIT ONE

Mirza Ghalib's Tomb
A poet's repose

Where Nizamuddin Basti
Open 6am-6pm

Takes you back to Ghalib's times

FAST FACT Ghalib's Haveli, p16

Can the 19th-century Urdu poet Mirza Ghalib have a resting place worthy of his iconic status? Impossible perhaps. The Mughal-era poet's stature is far too majestic. With his verses figuring in literary works, pop music and bestselling books, the poet is a popular cultural icon.

Ghalib's tomb complex covers an area of 3,500 sq ft and is tucked away in Nizamuddin Basti, a densely populated Muslim locality. Renovated in 2009, it gives a sense of the times in which Ghalib lived. The courtyard is paved with red sandstone, white marble inlays and ornamental patterns. A delicate hand-carved stone lattice screen shields it from the street. A Ghalib couplet is inscribed on a marble slab. Next door is Chausanth Khamba; don't miss it.

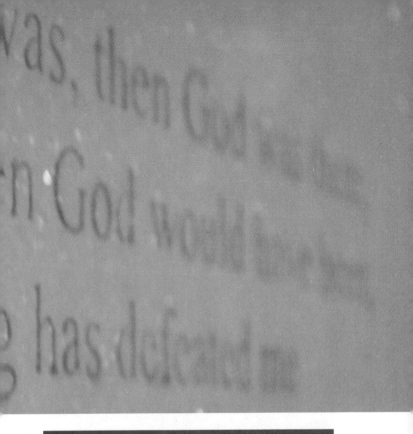

vas, then God ...
...n God would ...
...g has defeated me

73

Chausanth Khamba
Magic in marble

Where Nizamuddin Basti
Open Sunrise to sunset

Rare Jehangir-era monument

The most beautiful of all buildings in the congested Nizamuddin Basti, it is also the most ignored. Most visitors to this 14th-century village, named after a Sufi saint, head straight to his shrine. A few notice Urdu poet Mirza Ghalib's tomb. Hidden behind this mausoleum is the marbled Chausanth Khamba (circa 1624), the rare Jehangir-era monument in Delhi, so well-preserved that it does not look old.

Built by Mirza Aziz Kokaltash, a foster brother of Emperor Akbar, Chausanth Khamba is so named because 64 pillars are said to support its roof. But you will only count 36. These join the roof in a soft, sloping harmony. The hall

has 10 tombs, two of which belong to Kokaltash and his wife. The rest could be of other family members. Since the walls have stone jaalis, sunlight falls through the latticework making embroidered patterns on the marble floor and tombs. Outside, towards the Ghalib memorial, there are more tombs.

Chausanth Khamba faces the open courtyard of Urs Mahal, a venue for cultural shows, which remains empty except in the evening when boys come to play cricket. Ghalib's tomb, too, is usually bare. Amid the desolation, the monument feels completely isolated, yet it is so close to civilization.

Surrounded by the basti's jagged skyline, the sound from the nearby alleys—children crying, women laughing, hawkers yelling, men arguing, pressure cookers whistling—wafts into the pillared hall where it echoes softly. You feel meditative and far from worldly temptations..

75

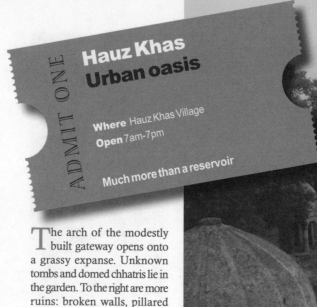

Hauz Khas
Urban oasis

ADMIT ONE

Where Hauz Khas Village
Open 7am-7pm

Much more than a reservoir

The arch of the modestly built gateway opens onto a grassy expanse. Unknown tombs and domed chhatris lie in the garden. To the right are more ruins: broken walls, pillared halls and dark corridors.

They face a lake—the focal point of Hauz Khas. In the early 14th century, Emperor Allauddin Khilji made a water reservoir here for the people of nearby Siri, the second city of Delhi.

As the Khilji dynasty faded away and their capital fell to ruins, the reservoir filled with silt. It was re-excavated by another Delhi ruler, Firoz Shah Tughlaq, who added a madrasa and mosque.

It is fitting that Tughlaq's tomb (1388), a domed structure measuring 13.56 sq m, soars above the rest of the ruins. One of the most elegant sites in Delhi, the madrasa's principal hall has delicately carved balconies and kiosks projecting out to the lake.

The Khilji-era chronicler Barni compared it to 'the palaces of ancient Babylon'. Delhi poet

Mutahhar of Kara found it 'a soul-animating courtyard'.

However, if history feels too oppressive, forget the past and just hang out in the balconies (careful, they don't have a barricade) and listen to the fluttering of pigeons. Look out over the forest and lake and spot the ducks paddling placidly on the water. Listen to your voice echoing off the walls of Tughlaq's tomb.

Since parts of the ruin have been completely destroyed, the stone stairs lead up and down to nothing; sometimes ending in thin air.

SOUTH DELHI

This was the palace of Muhammad bin Tughlaq, a sultan who was so eccentric that he forcibly moved Delhi's entire population 700 miles south to the Deccan. Having survived many transformations, Bijay Mandal, or what is left of it, is like difficult poetry with the first and last verses missing.

Historians call it Delhi's most puzzling building. They guess it was the site of the famous thousand-pillared hall; the pillars were of painted wood and the roof exquisitely carved. But all that is gone.

Hardly anyone climbs the stairs to reach the plinth on which the palace was built during the first half of the 14th century. The main hall is open to the elements yet is dark and musty. Its southern portion has collapsed. Its walls have lost their smoothness, the roof is broken. The hall has two treasure pits from which pearls, porcelain, gold and rubies were excavated during the last century.

There is an octagonal pavilion on the roof. But the ramp that leads up ends in a

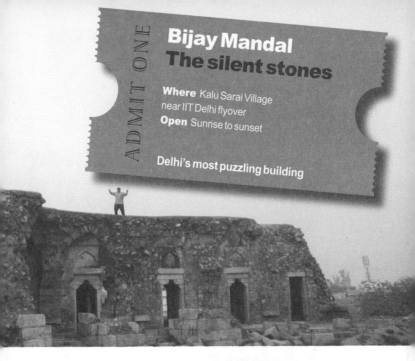

ADMIT ONE

Bijay Mandal
The silent stones

Where Kalu Sarai Village
near IIT Delhi flyover
Open Sunrise to sunset

Delhi's most puzzling building

padlocked door. Daring boys climb the walls for a majestic view of the city, but don't risk it. The northern view from the main hall is of a burial ground, which houses the shrine of a Sufi saint called Sheikh Hasan Tahir.

Beyond it is an arcaded building. The other side is not as scenic and offers a peek into the private lives of the residents of Begumpur village. You hear the barking of dogs from the bungalows of Sarvapriya Vihar. But the silence of the stones overpowers everything.

79

SOUTH DELHI

ADMIT ONE

**Begumpuri Masjid
Prayerless whispers**

Where Begumpur Village
Sarvapriya Vihar, near IIT Delhi
Open Sunrise to sunset

Tourists are rare in this imposing ruin

FAST FACT A 14th-century mosque with magnificent domes and pillars

You do not expect such a vast arcaded courtyard to appear as you climb the short flight of stairs from the entrance. This mid-14th-century mosque is simple and rundown, yet grand. The pillars are massive, but few designs are etched on the arches and columns.

Raised on a plinth, the mosque's chief entrance on the eastern side, faces the haphazard skyline of Begumpuri Village, which is easy to ignore once you enter. The calm surrounding the courtyard makes the congested world outside seem unreal.

The magnificent domes take you aback completely. There are 44 domed compartments on three sides. The Mecca-facing western side has a prayer chamber as well as the building's central arch, bordered by sloping buttresses with in-built winding staircases. Feel free to climb them. The view of the courtyard clashes with that of the village—clotheslines, water tanks and cow dung patties.

Believed to be built by a Tughlaq-era minister called Khan Jahan Junan Shah, Begumpuri Masjid probably served as the principal Friday

mosque during the reign of Muhammad bin Tughlaq.

During the anarchic times of 18th-century Delhi, defenseless communities moved inside the mosque and a village sprung up. This was cleared by the Archaeological Survey of India in the 1920s.

Today the mosque is dead. Prayers have been discontinued, the walls are broken, parts of the roof have collapsed and the stonework is blackened. Goats graze, chickens squawk, village boys play cricket and lovers scrawl 'I love you' messages. Rarely visited by tour groups, the absence of touts and souvenir sellers makes an excursion here more intense than in Delhi's other popular ruins.

SOUTH DELHI

Malai Mandir
Little Tamil Nadu

Where R.K. Puram
Open 6.30am-noon, 5pm-9pm
(opens 7am, Nov-Feb)

The temple's main deity is Karthik

FAST FACT The main temple is built of blue granite

Ethnic groups from other parts of the country have made this capital city their home, adding richness to its culture. The last stop of Delhi's Tamil community, Sree Uttara Swami Malai Mandir is situated on a hillock (malai means 'mountain' in Tamil). North India ends at its entrance gate. No, at the shoe rack, which keeps Tamil newspapers.

The courtyard buzzes with the musical sound of Tamil.

Men sport white veshtis; women have fragrant gajras woven into their hair. Here you witness the joys of traditional family life. Mothers run after little children, newly married couples take each other's pictures and old people eat the holy prasad.

The wedding scene of Shiva is painted on the backdrop of the stage in the courtyard used for cultural events. Shiva's son Karthik is the temple's main deity.

82

The shrine at the foot of the hill is dedicated to Shiva, though there are other gods beside the silver-plated lingam. The black statue of Goddess Meenakshi is always dressed in bright Kanjeevaram sarees.

Midway up the hill, is the Adi Shankaracharya hall, the venue for assemblies. Near the top is a little shrine dedicated to the snake god and milk is offered on its hood.

The main temple on the hilltop was built in 1973 from blue granite. Showing south Indian influences from the Chola era, the walls are sculpted with the images of gods.

Unfortunately, climbing so high doesn't offer any majestic scenery. The view of the residential neighbourhoods of R.K. Puram and Vasant Vihar is disappointing. However, the hill's slope is taken over by pink bougainvilleas that make for a lovely sight.

83

SOUTH DELHI

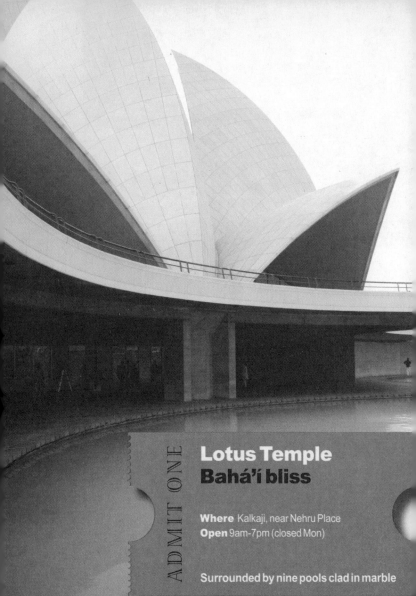

ADMIT ONE

Lotus Temple
Bahá'í bliss

Where Kalkaji, near Nehru Place
Open 9am-7pm (closed Mon)

Surrounded by nine pools clad in marble

Short of Scientology, Delhi has houses of worship of almost every religion and sect. The Lotus Temple is one of only eight temples in the world dedicated to the Bahá'í faith, a relatively new religion, the followers of which are persecuted in their prophet's land, Iran.

Built over six years and opened to the people in 1986, the temple is so popular that it has been rated as one of the most-visited monuments in the world. During certain periods, its visitors surpassed those of the Taj Mahal and Eiffel Tower. The reason behind its wild popularity may be its award winning design.

The temple's 27 lotus-shaped petals are fashioned out of white concrete. Surrounded by nine pools, their exteriors are clad in white Greek marble panels.

But the chief prayer hall is the temple's best feature. There are no statues or images, neither is any ritual allowed inside. With a capacity of 1,300 people, the worship room is manned by attendants who request that you don't talk. The resulting silence might be forced, but after a while you start feeling a bit meditative and begin to enjoy the atmosphere.

The hall's marble floor is spotlessly clean and the glass-panelled walls make it glow superbly in the natural daylight. When the sun sets, the electric bulbs shoot up light rays from within its petals, making the temple one of the most beautiful sights in Delhi at night.

FAST FACT The temple is one of only eight in the world dedicated to the Bahá'í faith

SOUTH DELHI

Mehrauli

ADMIT ONE

Qutub Minar
379 steps to heaven

Where Mehrauli
Open 6am-6pm

India's highest stone tower (72.5m)

Qutub Minar

Mughal Masjid

Adam Khan's Tomb

Hijron ka Khanqah

Jahaz Mahal

Mehrauli Archaeological Park

Khirki Masjid

Tughlaqabad Fort

Chhattarpur Temples

Size matters, and sometimes adversely. Lightning has twice damaged the Qutub Minar, India's highest stone tower. This five-storeyed red-and-buff sandstone tower, with marble trimmings higher up, massaged the ego of three early Islamic rulers: Qutubuddin Aibak who laid the foundation and supervised the construction of the first storey in the 12th century; Iltutmish who built the second, third and fourth storeys; and Firoz Shah Tughlaq, who built the fifth storey stretching the minar to its present height of 72.5 m. The British too made their addition – the balustrades that surround the balconies are Gothic.

As part of the Quwwatul Islam mosque, it is no surprise that Quranic inscriptions cover the walls of the Qutub Minar. Some historians believe it was named after Qutubuddin Aibak who commissioned the tower. Others think that it was named after Bakhtiyar Kaki, the Sufi saint popularly known as Qutub Sahib, whose shrine lies in the same neighbourhood. The Sufis say the tower is symbolic of Kaki's staff and that it connects earth to heaven. If that is true, then this is the shortest route to heaven—just 379 steps.

MEHRAULI

Alas, the entry is closed for safety reasons. But that doesn't discourage the heaven-seekers. In 2006, the Qutub Minar received more visitors than the Taj Mahal. While the Qutub Minar itself looms large, its complex has other equally engaging distractions. There are mosques, tombs, gateways and gardens.

As Delhi's first grand mosque of the late 12th century, **Quwwatul Islam** (above) was made from the rubble of Hindu and Jain temples that the conquerors destroyed after driving the Hindu rulers out of Delhi in 1192.

The mosque's columns and pillars are elaborately carved with disfigured Hindu idols. Tourists walk under the lofty arches and pose against tombs, not caring that they are in the midst of a graveyard of ancient conflicts. It gives the illusion that the past is dead.

Alai Darwaza, a gateway built by Alauddin Khilji, was the chief entrance to the mosque. Elaborately decorated with Quranic inscriptions and floral motifs, this mix of red sandstone and white marble is among Delhi's most beautiful gateways. The iron pillar in the mosque's courtyard dates from the 4th century and miraculously shows no signs of rust.

Not far away is the tomb of **Iltutmish**. Its walls are thick and the interiors are carved with calligraphy and floral motifs. If you are in awe of the supposed invincibility of emperors, turn to **Alai Minar**.

Commissioned by Khilji, it was intended to be double the Qutub Minar's size. However, it's just a 25m-high heap of stones, since it could not be completed. The emperor died prematurely and he too has a tomb in the complex, although the grave is missing.

89

MEHRAULI

Mughal Masjid
Leafy retreat

Where Qutub Minar Complex, Mehrauli
Open 6am-6pm

Unembellished beauty

Delhi's most heartbreakingly beautiful mosque, it is inside the Qutub Minar complex. With three onion-shaped domes, it is small, its two minarets look frail, and it faces a little walled garden. Built during the late Mughal times when Mehrauli was a favoured summer refuge for royalty, its beauty lies in its sparseness. There is no carving or sculpture—not even a bit of marble—just rubble masonry. The decorative work on the entrance arches is concealed behind coats of paint.

The original gateway to the south is closed and the present entrance is through an opening in the east wall.

Set against the glorious

Qutub Minar, the mosque goes largely unnoticed. But its solitude adds to its character.

A large neem tree leans over the central dome and the stone courtyard smells leafy with mulberry, pomegranate, guava and gular (ficus) trees. The cracks on the weathered structure give an illusion of Quranic inscriptions.

The white-walled prayer chamber, which has three compartments, remains amazingly quiet considering the heavy tourist traffic outside.

The sole window opens onto the lane through which tourists pass on their way to the Qutub Minar. Those who spot the quiet mosque are the lucky ones.

FAST FACT A walled garden

91

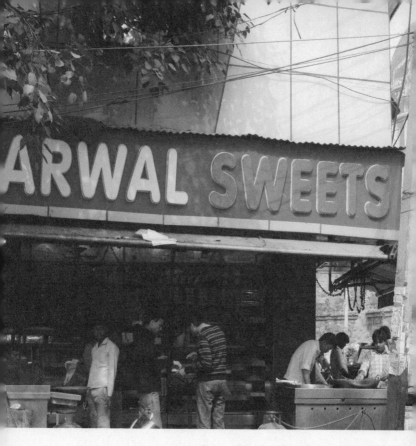

Standing on a hilly mound, this structure is more than just the ruined tomb of Adam Khan, a scheming foster brother of Akbar whom the Mughal emperor punished by having him hurled repeatedly from a parapet until he died.

The circa 1562 octagonal structure is also known as Bhool Bhullaiya, or a place where one may get lost, since its thick walls enclose a maze of passageways. It looks onto a bazaar and a bus terminal, the part of the historic district of Mehrauli that seems least historic.

Walk up to the tomb to find yourself amid the quiet charms of Indian life. Grannies pick their noses on the stairs;

FAST FACT Akbar executed Adam Khan by hurling him from a parapet

ADMIT ONE

Adam Khan's Tomb
Bhool Bhullaiya

Where Opposite Mehrauli bus terminal
Open Sunrise to sunset

Encloses a maze of passageways

jobless boys snooze against the pillars; old men talk politics atop the boundary wall; stray dogs prowl in the corridor and the homeless enjoy their siesta hour. There is also a view of the Qutub Minar.

Bhool Bhullaiya, made of grey sandstone and rubble masonry, is one of the few Akbar-era monuments in Delhi.

The dome is crowned by a red sandstone finial. The circular verandah has three arches on each of its eight sides, and eight arched entrances open into the dark chamber.

Adam Khan lies in the centre, his grave absurdly narrow.

It is said that his mother was also buried here, but her tomb is missing.

93

MEHRAULI

Hijron ka Khanqah
Hijras' resting place

Where Mehrauli Bazaar,
opp. Mangla Electronics
Open 8am-8pm

Sufi retreat for eunuchs

Beautifully maintained, surprisingly serene, and almost always empty, this is a Sufi spiritual retreat for hijras, or eunuchs, who beg for money by flaunting their ambiguous sexuality, and yet are fiercely guarded about their private lives.

Situated on the scenic bazaar street, the khanqah is entered through an iron grill. Up a flight of six stairs, the courtyard is covered with 50 whitewashed tombs. Forty-nine hijras are buried here. The chief tomb, covered by a roof, is said to be that of the sister of a man known simply as Sheikh Baba. This was originally a Lodhi-era graveyard that was claimed by eunuchs at the turn of the 20th

century. The western wall has seven mihrab (niches), indicating the direction of Mecca's main shrine. Try climbing the stairs —the view of the courtyard from the roof is lovely.

Kinnars, the politically correct term for hijras, come here from various neighbourhoods of Delhi, as well as from regions as far as Haryana, Punjab, Andhra Pradesh and Maharashtra. They arrive in groups, big and small, usually to celebrate an occasion. Here they feast, sing, dance and pray.

Sometimes they cook in the graveyard or they even bring in packed biryani. In their absence, the khanqah with its giant neem tree remains as still as a grave.

FAST FACT Lovely rooftop views

95

MEHRAULI

Jahaz Mahal
Marooned palace

Where At the end of Mehrauli Bazaar, close to Hauz-e-Shamsi
Open Sunrise to sunset

Hosts the floral festival, Phoolwalon ki Sair

Every year after the monsoons, this ravaged monument whose name means 'ship palace', plays host to music, dance and acting. It becomes the focal point of cultural activities marking Phoolwalon ki Sair, a festival in which floral tributes are paid to two premier Hindu and Muslim shrines in the Mehrauli area.

Some historians say Jahaz Mahal, built during the Lodhi period (1452-1526), was a mosque. Some think it was the residence of a holy man. Others believe it to be a serai (inn) that took in visiting pilgrims. Owing to its proximity to Hauz-e-Shamsi, a water tank built by Sultan Iltutmish, it could also have been a pleasure palace, a harem, or a summer refuge for the Delhi royalty. In any case, Jahaz Mahal got its name because its reflection in the rippling waters of the tank looked like a moving ship.

Over the years the lake was reduced to a filthy pond and the mahal lost its reflection. It also lost its southern wall. Most of the blue ceramic tiles on the domed pavilion over the central gateway were lost. Yet there is beauty in this dilapidation. The chhatris show delicate carvings. The mihrab on the western wall indicates a mosque. The arched chambers promise serenity.

And the southern wall's collapse has its bright side: it has opened the courtyard's view to a lively park.

FAST FACT Jahaz Mahal's reflection in the rippling waters of the tank looked like a moving ship

MEHRAULI

Delhi would still do fine if it had no monuments, except those in Mehrauli Archaeological Park. Spread over 100 acres, the hilly green space in the southern edge of the capital has 70 monuments covering almost everything—tombs, mosques, caravanserais, gardens, gateways, follies—and from almost every period. There are the Lal Kot walls of the pre-Islamic times, the Qutub Minar (right next door) of the Slave Dynasty, tombs of the Lodhi period (above), pavilions of the Mughal period and follies of the British.

The **Jamali Kamali** mosque and tomb—the park's principal attraction—combines two dynasties. A poet, both in Sikander Lodhi's and Humayun's courts, Sheikh Fazlullah, aka Jamali Kamali, built his own tomb in 1528.

A rare Delhi monument having retained almost perfectly

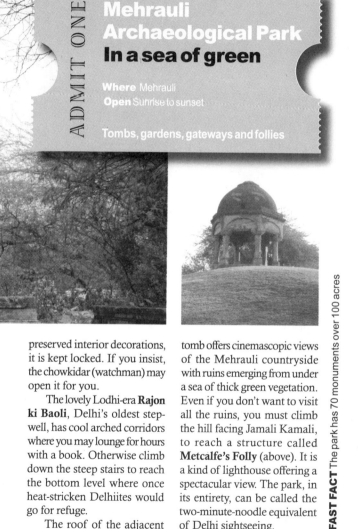

Mehrauli Archaeological Park
In a sea of green

Where Mehrauli
Open Sunrise to sunset

Tombs, gardens, gateways and follies

preserved interior decorations, it is kept locked. If you insist, the chowkidar (watchman) may open it for you.

The lovely Lodhi-era **Rajon ki Baoli**, Delhi's oldest step-well, has cool arched corridors where you may lounge for hours with a book. Otherwise climb down the steep stairs to reach the bottom level where once heat-stricken Delhiites would go for refuge.

The roof of the adjacent tomb offers cinemascopic views of the Mehrauli countryside with ruins emerging from under a sea of thick green vegetation. Even if you don't want to visit all the ruins, you must climb the hill facing Jamali Kamali, to reach a structure called **Metcalfe's Folly** (above). It is a kind of lighthouse offering a spectacular view. The park, in its entirety, can be called the two-minute-noodle equivalent of Delhi sightseeing.

FAST FACT The park has 70 monuments over 100 acres

99

MEHRAULI

ADMIT ONE

Khirki Masjid
Ravaged domes

Where Khirki Village,
opposite MGF Mall, Saket
Open Sunrise to sunset

Named for its khirkis, or latticed windows

With its blackened walls, collapsed domes, and a covered hall in which light plays hide and seek, this is Delhi's most romantic ruin. One of the seven mosques built in the 1370s by Khan-i-Jahan Junan Shah, prime minister to Firoz Shah Tughlaq, the marvel got its name from the red sandstone latticed windows, or khirkis, that line its walls.

A domed sloping tower guards each of the four corners. Tapering minarets flank the domed gateways at the centre of each side. The pillared hall, with 25 squares, is the highlight. A jumble of arches and domes, it takes its dim light from the khirkis, as well as four courtyards. The Mecca-facing western wall has no window and is dark and musty. The bats hanging from the ceiling make a 'chee-chee' sound that echoes off the pillars.

The roof, accessible by staircases on the eastern gateway, has 72 domes (nine have collapsed). They are rendered more beautiful by the juxtaposition of the surrounding skyline of the Khirki village, which grabs attention with its breathtaking ugliness. Across the road is the MGF Mall, a striking contrast to the village.

MEHRAULI

ADMIT ONE

Tughlaqabad Fort
Forsaken citadel

Where Mehrauli-Badarpur Road
Open Sunrise to sunset
(early morning hours are best)

Built to repel the Mongols who never came

Think frozen music. The Tughlaqabad Fort's sloping rubble-filled outer walls spread out on a hillock, are like ripples of sound waves extending to infinity. The third city of Delhi (circa 1324) lies forsaken. Monkeys have taken over the ramparts. Thorny grass has laid siege to palace enclosures.

Built in just two years by the Tughlaq dynasty founder, Ghiasuddin, the fort's walls with their invincible fortifications of arrow slots and tiers of loopholes, were designed to

All that has disappeared. There is no water in the seven tanks. Most of the 13 outer gates are blocked by jungle growth. The underground pits and arched passageways of the citadel are home to snakes and wild peacocks.

After Ghiasuddin's death in a freak accident (he was inside a pavilion when it collapsed on him), his successor, Muhammad bin Tughlaq forced Tughlaqabad's population to move to his new capital in central India. The fort fell into disrepair and acquired all the trappings of an abandoned place. Some believe that Tughlaqabad Fort was cursed by Delhi's Sufi saint Hazrat Nizamuddin Auliya. Having a strained relationship with Ghiasuddin, he had said, 'Ya rahey ujjar, ya basey gujjar' (May the fort remain desolate, or else be occupied by herdsmen).

With its massive circular towers and colossal bastions built to last for an eternity, the fort's desolation seems especially melancholic.

Tourists rarely visit here, although it is definitely worth the trip. Its savageness will stay with you long after you have left its seemingly unassailable ramparts.

repel the Mongol invaders who never came. Inside was a city with a palace and citadel for the king, and neighbourhoods and bazaars for his people. The 14th-century traveller Ibn Batuta talked of 'gilded tiles' and 'vast stores of wealth'.

FAST FACT Some believe that Tughlaqabad Fort was cursed by Hazrat Nizamuddin Auliya

MEHRAULI

ADMIT ONE

Chhattarpur Temples
Holy expanse

Where Off Mehrauli-Gurgaon Road
Open Morning to night

Dedicated to Adya Katyayani

Spread over 60 acres, this is Hinduism at its showy best. Known as Chhattarpur Mandir, the Adya Katyayani temple compound grew to its massive size of three complexes over successive years. Lying off the Mehrauli-Gurgaon Road, it is a brave attempt to compensate for the absence of Hindu heritage monuments in Delhi, most of which comprise almost entirely Muslim-built mosques, palaces, forts and tombs.

Established in 1974 by Baba Sant Nagpal, a holy man with influence in Delhi's power circles, the temple's regulars included late Prime Minister Indira Gandhi. Dedicated to an avatar of Durga, but also home to various other gods, the complex has dozens of sculpted tigers and lions guarding the walls, pillars, stairs, and gardens.

The snow-white shikhars (towers) in the main Shaktipeeth

temple are hidden behind the light brown façade of Utsav Mandapam, a hall used during festivals. One of the six shrines has a black Nandi bull on a chessboard-patterned floor. Silver-plated walls in Ram's temple complement the ornate marble pillars. The biggest hall, with colourfully painted domes, is devoted to Shiva-Parvati. The courtyard has a counter where one can arrange a blessing for newly acquired cars (light vehicles Rs 250, heavy vehicles Rs 350).

Next door is the sprawling Lakshmi Vinayak temple, inspired by classical south Indian temple architecture; the chief idols—Lakshmi and Ganesha—are of pure silver. Its doorway is capped by a painting of Baba Nagpal sleeping inside a python's mouth.

The langar hall in the basement can accommodate around 5,000 devotees.

MEHRAULI